MICRONESIAN
HANDICRAFT BOOK
OF THE
TRUST TERRITORY
OF THE
PACIFIC ISLANDS

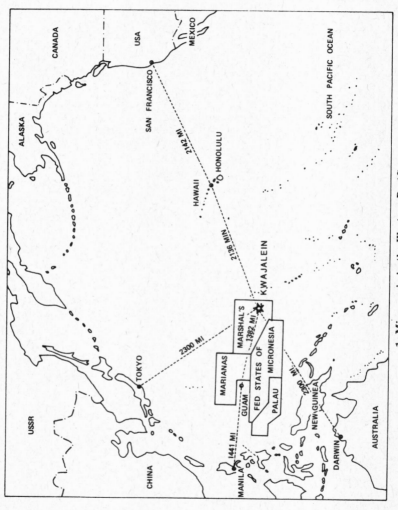

1. Micronesia in the Western Pacific

MICRONESIAN HANDICRAFT BOOK OF THE TRUST TERRITORY OF THE PACIFIC ISLANDS

BY
MARJORIE D. WELLS

A Hearthstone Book

Carlton Press, Inc.   New York, N.Y.

Dedication

This book dedication goes first to Mary Lanwi, Majuro, Marshall Islands, for her untiring efforts to keep the handicraft arts from becoming extinct. Then to Rose McWhelung, who has worked so hard to keep interest alive in the crafts in Ponape. Also to Inobou on Palau and others there who have purchased and exported the heavy story-boards and all the carvings. Now to the many Women's Clubs in the Marshalls, Mariana, and Caroline Islands, whose talents and deft fingers have made the lovely handicrafts and are continuing to do so. Very importantly, this is also dedicated to the men, all over the Territory, who carve, weave, make coconut dolls or engage in whatever other crafts they may be talented enough to execute. To all of you, all Micronesians everywhere, go our grateful thanks for keeping the handicraft arts alive in Micronesia. May God grant you the enthusiasm to continue. This book is a record for you of the pleasure and beauty you give to others with your crafts.

2. Mary Lanwi, Majuro, Marshall Islands.

Contents

Index of Illustrations

Preface

This is Micronesian handicraft from the Trust Territory of the Pacific Islands. Micronesia means 'the small islands' that are scattered over an area of about three million square miles in the Western Pacific Ocean, north of the equator. Measuring from east to west, the distance is about 2,765 miles, or approximately the same distance as that across the continental United States of America. There are ninety-six island groups, atolls and single islands. The land area of this vast territory covers only six-hundred and eighty-seven square miles. In the ninety-six island groups, there are approximately two thousand tiny islands. Micronesia includes the Marshalls, the Marianas and the Caroline Islands.

The United States administers the Trust Territory as a Strategic Trust for the United Nations. A system, based on the plan of government of the United States, is used. This includes three branches of government: executive, legislative, and judicial. There are six administration districts: Marshalls, Marianas, Palau, Ponape, Yap, and Truk, with the capital located on Saipan in the Marianas.

Acknowledgments

To my husband, Walter, whose moral and technical support made this book possible I owe much thanks. To the rest of my family for their support and encouragement—Gram, Greg, and Cindy—also goes my appreciation. I owe a debt of gratitude to the wonderful Micronesian Shop Committee who helped me learn to appreciate the beautiful crafts of Micronesia: Sonny Ogden, Patty Arnold, Ethel Boniface, Addie Johnson, Tranni Quinn, Imogene Brambley, Gloria Muirhead, and Gilda Sternfels. To our wonderful girl Friday, Sarai Boitoing, the whole family says thank you. For Helen Elliott's final editing and to Mary Griffin for her many hours of slide editing, my grateful thanks. To my cousin, professional photographer Carl Merrifield, who has spent many hours producing black and white glossies from colored slides: *kommol kwo kannuij emmol* (thank you very much). Finally, much loves goes to my mother, Corene Merrifield, to my sister, Madonna, and to my late father, Herbert Dean Merrifield, for their endowment to me of a special love and caring for people and for the legacy of a constant and abiding faith in our Lord, which strengthens me daily.

May these legends become favorites for Nick to read to Nicky and Andy.

Introduction

Trust Territory of the Pacific Islands' Changing Status

Known as Micronesia, the Trust Territory of the Pacific Islands has been a single entity since 1946 when it was first made a Strategic Trust of the United States of America by the United Nations. Through the years the United States has prepared it as much as possible for future self-governing powers. Hopefully, for continued cooperation and for stability from United States monetary support in a situation of mutual benefit to both areas, this will continue to be a very close association.

The Mariana Islands, which are located south of Japan and north of Guam have become a United States Commonwealth, effective in 1981, with full U.S. citizenship status to be granted upon temination of the Trustee Agreement. Their capital is located in Saipan, NMI (The Commonwealth of the Northern Mariana Islands.)

The government of the Marshall Islands, located in Majuro, Marshall Islands, is established as a constitutional one modeled after the British parliamentary system. They rejected a union with the rest of Micronesia on the first of May, 1979. It has a president in place of a prime minister and a single parliament (Nitijela). They have negotiated a free association status with the United States, thus retaining their political sovereignty, while granting certain defense privileges to the United States Government in a mutual agreement for the U.S. continuing services and some budgetary support.

The Federated States of Micronesia include Yap, Truk, Ponape, and Kosrae formerly (Kusaie), all located in the Caroline Islands and forming the central area across Micronesia. The Federated States of Micronesia adopted their constitution on the twelfth of July, 1978. Palau and the Marshalls rejected this constitution. FSM is headquarted in Ponape, Caroline Islands, headed by a president, who is elected by their single house of congress. The FSM is also negotiating a free political status agreement with the United States. The United States will be responsible for the defense of the Islands.

Finally, on July 9, 1980, Palau held its third plebiscite and adopted a new constitution. Their new government, scheduled to be installed January 1, 1981, is to be a constitutional government with a bi-cameral (two party) legislature, and headed by a President. Their president will be elected by the people and not by the congress as is the policy of the FSM. Palau is also negotiating a free status with the United States, but they are also desirous of continued defense support and monetary support.

A free association is an arrangement whereby in return for certain budgetary, postal and aviation services the United States will retain exclusive rights to use certain areas for military purposes along with the right to deny access for military purposes to other countries. It will be an agreement which can be terminated by either party. There will be a popular vote taken, known as a plebiscite, with U.N. observers following all of the signings of the approved negotiations.

Hundreds of American families have spent time in Micronesia and have a special love and rapport with the islanders that lasts a lifetime and is indescribably beautiful. We hope they will be very pleased with their new status.

MICRONESIAN HANDICRAFT BOOK OF THE TRUST TERRITORY OF THE PACIFIC ISLANDS

Marshall Islands
District

Today, Majuro serves as the eastern gateway to Micronesia. The 727 jets of Air Micronesia land on the tiny coral air strips and serve the far flung islands of Micronesia, arriving on Majuro, Marshall Islands, from Hawaii, twenty-five hundred miles to the northeast.

The tiny land area of the Marshalls is approximately 69.84 square miles, on 1,150 tiny islands, on atolls, and on islets known as table reefs. This 69.84 square miles supports a population of nearly nineteen thousand Marshallese. Non-Micronesians are not allowed to own land in the Trust Territory. The Marshalls are scattered over 180,000 square miles of the Western Pacific Ocean.

About forty percent of all Micronesian copra exported is produced in the Marshall Islands. It is with great logistical and transport difficulties that they accomplish this because of the vast area of water it is necessary to navigate. Much handicraft is produced for air or sea shipment to Kwajalein and Guam. Very little is exported out of the Trust Territory due to the high tariff imposed by the United States Government on handicraft items imported for resale. This tariff should be removed to help the Micronesians become more self-supporting by enlarging their handicraft market.

Bikini, Eniwetok, and Kwajalein, three areas that are well known to many in the United States, are all located in the Marshalls. The more than eleven-hundred islands are located in two partially parallel chains, running north and south. The western chain is known as Ralik, the Marshallese word for sunset, while the eastern chain is known as Ratak, Marshallese for sunrise.

Kili Bags-Marshall Islands

When the United States began preparations to test the atomic bomb in the Western Pacific, they found that Bikini, at the Northern end of the Ralik chain in the Marshalls, seemed, with its one-hundred and sixty-six inhabitants, to have the maximum space available for testing with the minimum number of Micronesians requiring displacement. They requested the Bikini people to move to nearby Rongerik Atoll, an uninhabited spot except for the ghost of Libokra, a bygone lengendary witch. According to legend, she stole Rongerik from its original location and hid it in its present site. Micronesians have many tales of the moving of islands, believed to have been originated mostly by island sailors who lost their navigational ability on some occasion and missed the island they were looking for. Therein would hang a new tale of supernatural movings. It was believed that the Bikini people would not take Libokra's legend seriously, after hundreds of years, but they did. She was said to have great power to concoct poisons to stunt the growth of the fruits of the coconut and pandanus trees, and to cause the fish in the lagoon to be inedible. The Bikini people were not surprised therefore when the food was neither palatable nor available, causing them to almost starve. After a few months they requested an immediate move to a more habitable island. They were resettled in temporary housing on Kwajalein, then moved to the uninhabited island of Kili in the Southern Marshalls. Kili does not have a lagoon, but rather stands alone, a table reef in the ocean, only slightly more than one-third square mile in area. Four months of the year it is almost isolated when the trade winds blow too strongly for the field trip boats to anchor in the rough ocean. Even when the tiny freighter is able to anchor, a small motor boat must be used to ferry in the supplies and pick up Kili's handicrafts and copra to be transported and marketed.

It is here, on tiny Kili Island, that the most beautiful handbags in the world are made. The lining of a Kili bag is woven of the tender green coconut palm leaf, unwound by hand from the tree, before it unfurls to begin its growth. The outside is prepared pandanus leaves, which have been bleached to natural white fiber strips and woven tightly with exquisite precision. The small rectangular purse measures four and one-half by seven inches and is five inches deep. Each handbag has a matched top. Our Marshall Islands handicraft co-ordinator told me that it takes a woman two weeks to prepare and weave the small bag, and four weeks to make the six by twelve-inch rectangular one that is about ten inches deep. The Bikini people are praised by all American women who are fortunate enough to obtain a Kili bag. The Kili bag comes in other sizes and shapes, but the ones described above are the most sought after, followed in popularity by the six-inch square handbag, which is more rare.

Kini or Kinien—
Marshallese Sleeping Mats

Marshallese sleeping mats, Kini, are woven of coconut fiber embroidered with colored coconut fiber strands, in flower designs, and then trimmed with exotic borders.

3.

The Ejols (commoner) uses the above described mat for his sleeping comfort. The Iroij (king) or other sleeping mats designed for royalty, are more intricately made, with the design woven into the mat as it is made. An elaborately woven border in matching design is skillfully attached. The royal mats are not for sale but are sometimes given to special visiting guests and foreign friends by the Marshallese to show their special fondness for the recipient.

The Marshallese sleeping mats are woven on all the islands in the Marshalls for individual use, but those making their way to the outside world generally originate in Jaluit or Majuro.

The mats are rectangular and measure approximately three by six feet in size.

Kano
Marshallese Table Mats

Weaving artifacts of beauty is a Marshallese skill that is unsurpassed anywhere in the world. Pandanus is painstakingly prepared into long narrow strands and bleached white or dyed in many colors. Then it is woven around coconut ribs to create mats in many shapes and sizes. Round ones are the most common. Finishing touches of goldringer, snakeshead and monkeyface cowries provide an exquisite trim. I never saw a snakeshead (*cypraea caputserpentis L.*) on any mats for sale. Many are made, but they are for gifts to guests rather than for sale in the market. The money cowry (*cypraea*

4.

moneta L.), the goldringer *(cypraea annulus)* and the *cypraea moneta* with the purple lining, known as the monkeyface, are all used extensively in trim. An ice pick or a tiny drill is used to bore a minute hole through which a pandanus strand is wound to attach the cowry to the woven mat.

5.

Mats range in size from three inches in diameter to eighteen inches and can be useful or decorative as hot mats, place mats or wall hangings.

Green Coconut Baskets

From fresh green fronds unwound from the trunk of the coconut palm, the Micronesian women weave a plate to put their food on. One is made for each member of the family. Upon finishing the meal, the woven plate is simply tossed away.

This same type of weaving goes into baskets of all sizes and shapes for use in their daily living. They serve as a suitcase and as a food container when the Micronesian takes a sea voyage. I have often watched them board a freighter bent under the weight of the food in their baskets. It may contain a whole stalk of bananas, a large pandanus, several yams, and many limes and oranges. Oftentimes a few breadfruit are added to the loaded basket, evidence of its sturdiness.

Fancy Marshallese Baskets

Fancy sewing baskets, woven of pandanus around coconut ribs, are fashioned into many sizes and shapes. Some are trimmed in tortoise shell, while others may utilize a weaving art with the various kinds of cowries. The tops of many baskets are crocheted of pandanus fiber in intricate designs. Some weavers add borders of contrasting colors.

Basket sizes vary from tiny, three-inch diameter round ones to large ones fourteen inches in diameter and standing ten inches tall.

Other styles may be six to fourteen inches across, but very shallow. These are made to hold pie pans as servers, or to hold casseroles, and can really serve many, many useful purposes and also be very decorative. Some are so intricately woven that they make lovely wall hangings.

Colorful baskets are woven on most of the Marshall Islands, but Majuro, Arno, Jaluit and Ailinglaplap produce the greatest number for sale.

Belin
Shell Head Leis

Visting an island brings many rewards to the visitor, one of which is the custom of the host and hostess presenting their shell *(Belin)* head *leis* to you. These are made of sea and land snails woven into a coconut or pandanus band and frequently embelished with cat's eyes (from the Turban shell) and different kinds of cowry shells. Often they are trimmed with a wide, colored coconut fiber fringe.

The alu, a smaller version of the sea snail shell, is woven into intricate head leis in variegated brown and white shells.

Leis—Kenwa—and Shell Necklaces
Marshall Islands

Leis made in the Marshall Islands to wear around the neck (kenwa) are woven of all kinds of cowries and snails' shells. Leis are made in thick wide versions and strands of necklaces are made in many lengths and designs.

The Likiep Island women weave an elegant lei of sea snails, called likajjir lei (common white snail). This white lei is brilliant with many layers of snail shells woven into a beautiful creation resembling a plumeria flower lei.

Dozens of styles of shell necklaces are fashioned of cowry shells. The goldringer cowry *(cypraea annulus L.)*, ivory in color with a perfect gold ring imprinted on it, seems to be a favorite of the Marshallese. It ranges in size from one-quarter to three-quarters of an inch in length. Most of the Marshallese necklaces are made of goldringers.

The strawberry *(cypraea helvola L.)*, a deep red mottled in soft white flecks, is as beautiful as many gemstones. It is fairly rare and very tiny, growing to only about a quarter of an inch at maturity. The strawberry is found more on Majuro's outer islands, and the necklaces made from it are lovely.

Preferred by many, the snakeshead or brownie *(cypraea caputserpentis L.)* cowries range in size from a tiny quarter of an inch to one-inch lengths. The smallest ones are the best for dainty necklaces, but frequently one large brownie is used as a pendant on a goldringer or money cowry (*cypraea moneta L.*) The money cowry is yellow and about the same size as the goldringers. Some have a purple underlining and are called monkeyfaces. All small shiny cowries are beautiful gems for leis and necklaces.

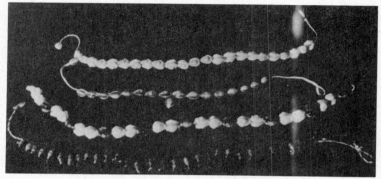

6.

7.

Belts
Kannir

A great variety of belts (kannir) are woven in the Marshall Islands. First formed out of woven coconut or pandanus wound around coconut rib, the belts are trimmed with elaborate shell work and crocheting. From Likiep comes an elegant woven kannir of money cowries. This is tightly strung on nylon fishing line, after tiny holes are drilled in each cowry shell. Cateyes and seeds, along with other cowries, are often crocheted into various designs. The belts are quite stiff, and a chain is crocheted of the pandanus fiber with the end fringed, which is then attached to the woven belt to be used as a tie, thus finishing the product.

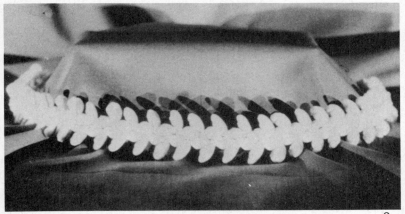

8.

Coconut Dolls
Ebeye—Marshall Islands

On Kwajalein Island, Wanjur works by day at the dock unloading boats and ships. At nights and on weekends he makes the only solid crafts of coconut that are made in the Marshall Islands, other than the carved canoes. Wanjur makes coconut dolls on Ebeye, where he lives.

He takes cleaned dried coconut (inner shell) from which the meat has been removed and polishes the nut with brown shoe polish to a high luster. Using a small coconut for the head and a larger one for the body, he attaches fiber from the inside of the coconut husk to the smaller nut and glues on shells for the eyes, nose and mouth. He applies small shells for the anatomy of the male doll and braids its hair, thus distinguishing it from the female doll, which has long, flowing fiber hair and properly placed shells. Wanjur weaves a tiny rope from the coconut fiber from inside the husk. From the rope he fashions legs and arms for the dolls. To the legs he adds tiny wooden feet for the finishing touch.

Shell Flowers
Marshall Islands

The Marshallese have made shell flowers for centuries, but we have only two in this collection. One is a small white flower, woven and crocheted together of sea snail shells and fastened to a tiger cowry (*cypraea tigris L.*), making a tiny bouquet.

The second one is of lovely white shells, woven and crocheted into a tiny corsage to be worn either as an ornament on a dress, or in the hair. But it looks spectacular on a Kili bag.

Crocheted Pandanus Fiber Flowers
Marshallese

Pandanus fiber is crocheted into exquisite flowers in all colors by the Marshallese. They make flowers representing many different kinds.

The fragile looking crocheted flower petals and leaves are shaped into flowers and attached to a bamboo twig. The twig

28

is then wound with green pandanus fiber to make a green stem to which the leaves are fastened.

These flowers are often used as a corsage or hair ornament. They make an elegant decoration for Kili bags or any kind of handbag.

9.

Marshallese Hats

Delicately woven white pandanus fiber hats are made for men, women and children on many of the Marshall Islands.

Fashioned with a wide brim and a narrow stiff serrated fringe trim of the fiber, the lady's hat has an intricate design woven into the crown, making each hat a work of art.

A narrow brimmed, high crowned version in the white pandanus fiber is made for men. Each can be worn with or without trim. The shell head leis make a striking addition to both the men's and women's hats, while a silk scarf also adds variety.

A work hat is woven of unbleached coconut fiber; both plain and interwoven with colored fibers, making interesting and decorative designs.

The Marshallese hats are very similar to the Panama hat.

10.

11.

Marshallese Fans

Colorful fans of varied sizes and shapes are created on many of the inhabited Marshall Islands.

Indescribably beautiful, the fans are crocheted of pandanus fiber of bright colors into intricate designs and then usually attached to genuine tortoise shell. Coconut fiber fringes of bright hues, or chicken feathers, plain or dyed, add the final trim. The fan handles are covered with the tightly woven pandanus in designs of beauty.

Pillow (Bit) Covers

Embroidery is another talent widely employed by the Marshallese women. Flower designs of close, bulky stitches are worked into white pillow cases. The designs stand out in bold relief and resemble freshly cut flowers.

Walking through a Marshallese village in early morning, one sees tiny flower gardens by each cottage in the form of the lovely embroidered covers stretched in the sun to dry.

Marshallese Purses
Nien Mani

Marshallese purses cover a wide spectrum of styles and sizes. Some resemble the multi-colored woven baskets with an intricate crocheted cover fashioned with cowries in many designs. A woven or braided handle is added. Frequently, four shells, attached by sewing to the bottom, form four little feet, thus avoiding soiling when set on the coral.

The nien mani (purses) are constructed by weaving prepared pandanus fiber strips around coconut frond ribs, then joined by hand sewing in an interlacing effect.

A child's tiny white handbag, measuring three inches in diameter by four inches tall, has an attached braided handle.

The most famous Marshallese purses are the Kili bags, previously described.

Cigarette Case
Jika or Jikarej Kej

Weaving patterned after the Kili bag construction is executed into a tiny appropriately shaped cigarette case, measuring two-and-one-quarter by four-and-one-half by one-and-one-half inches.

Two separate cases are woven: the inner of narrow strips of tightly woven coconut fiber, the outer side of very narrow pandanus fibers, tightly woven into plain and fancy designs, both white and colored.

The two holders are then fashioned into one piece by sewing the top edges together with the prepared fibers. The finished case consists of a top which slides over the bottom section to form a holder for a package of cigarettes.

Stick Charts of the Marshalls
Jat

Through the centuries, the Marshallese have been recognized as superb navigators. It is believed that they originally migrated to Micronesia from Mongolia or elsewhere in Southeast Asia by means of small outrigger canoes, at least six centuries ago. Settling on many islands, on atolls and on single table reef islands in the Ralik and Ratik chains, they continued to navigate as they island-hopped through the centuries.

Today, canoes are frequently reported lost in a storm-tossed sea, only to turn up in port later with all hands safe. Often the crew has been battered by winds and high seas, but

ATOLL LOCATION KEY
for
MARSHALLESE STICK CHART

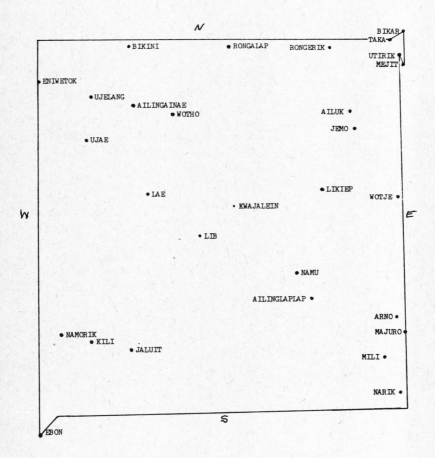

their navigational ability usually enables them to find shelter on a nearby island until the storm abates. They then sail back to their home port or on to their original destination. They read the currents in the sea, thus determining the correct manner in which to right their sails.

Some years ago, Mr. Raymond DeBrum, who lived on Likiep, gave a concise account of the Marshallese navigational skills to a radiological group which made a stop there. For that group he made a stick chart showing the currents as the Marshallese knew them. His account to this group is too

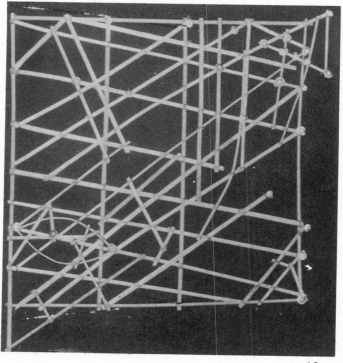

13.

lengthy to repeat in this book on crafts, but it may be obtained by visiting the Bishop Museum in Honolulu.

Today, a Marshallese stick chart is a handicraft item that is much sought after by visitors and temporary residents for its historical value and intricate work.

The stick chart, made of coconut ribs tied together with pandanus fibers, forms a map. Shells placed at strategic spots represent islands or groups of islands. Rib sticks are curved to show the currents of the ocean. These charts are made in many different sizes and shapes, representing both the Ralik and the Ratik chains. Some symbolize only a few islands, in one chain or the other.

For centuries the navigational secrets were kept within a family and handed down from generation to generation. Now long distance travel by canoe is not undertaken on the grand scale of years ago. Today the Marshallese travel on the larger motor-powered field trip boats or by airplane.

Today's charts are made as a craft for sale to collectors.

Outrigger Canoe Models
Marshall Islands

About six centuries ago, Asians are believed to have migrated in wa (outrigger canoes) to the tropical island paradises of Micronesia. They inhabited many islands on atolls and some table reef islets over an area of three million square miles in the Western Pacific Ocean. In this huge area you will find only seven-hundred square miles of land! The water area encompasses approximately the same area as the land mass of the continental United States.

In the southeastern part of this area, located ten degrees north of the equator and extending north for several-hundred miles, and west, lie the Ralik and Ratik chains of the lovely low coral reef Marshalls. First discovered by the English, both the Marshalls and the British Gilbertese people were known as Micronesians.

In excellent temperatures ranging from seventy-two to eighty-eight degrees, with a definite dry season and a rainy season, during which showers fall and the sun soon shines again, the dark-skinned friendly Marshallese people fish, make copra and fashion handicrafts. They live on many islands among the 1,150 tiny spots in the sea. The Marshall

Islands District covers 180,000 square miles of the Pacific Ocean, with a total land area of barely 69.84 square miles to support a population of over seventeen thousand people. About forty percent of the copra production of the Trust Territory of the Pacific (Micronesia) is produced in the Marshalls.

Today the Marshallese on the outer islands still use the outrigger canoe to navigate the wide Pacific from island to island and sometimes even from atoll to atoll. An atoll consists of many islands on a large coral reef, usually surrounding a lagoon. People living in district centers today tend to travel as passengers on field trip boats or airplanes instead of by canoe.

The model portrayed here depicts, the one-man Marshallese outrigger canoe that is still widely used on the outer islands.

14.

Yukwe Yuk Shirts—Jot
Mu—Jamoa—Mu

The Marshallese women wear their medium length dresses (nuknuk) fashioned with a full, gathered or pleated skirt. They also feature a low neckline.

Foreigners living in Micronesia enjoy wearing the loose fitting Hawaiian Mu Mu (jamoa). Both Micronesians and foreign guests enjoy bright Polynesian patterns and prints. The women sew their own dresses, their husbands' and sons' shirts (jot), and clothing for their daughters besides making shirts, mu mus and childrens' clothing for sale in the handicraft shops. Exotic cottons, nylons and polyesters are turned into colorful fashions.

Mu mus and shirts are included in this book because they are made without patterns for the most part, and represent an important craft—sewing. Matching shirt and dress sets are often given as going away presents by the Marshallese to foreign friends, who are permanently moving from the islands.

Coconut (Grass-Type) Skirts
Jaluit—Marshall Islands

From Jaluit comes a soft coconut fiber, grass-type skirt featuring a gaily woven two-inch-wide waistband. Thin ropes are crocheted of the fiber and attached to the waistband, which, when tied, hold the skirt securely around the waist.

The coconut fiber is made by processing the green coconut palm leaf through various steps of cutting, drying and bleaching, to obtain the soft white color of the long grass-like strands. These are used, in the soft white color, to make the skirts. Only the trim, which is woven of pandanus or coconut fibers into the waistband, is occasionally dyed in many colors.

These skirts are very rare. Princess Kabua, of Ebeye, once obtained twenty from Jaluit—the only ones for sale to outsiders while I lived in the Islands. These are exquisitely made and very soft to the touch.

Shell On Wood Picture Frame
and
Marshallese Vase

Many Marshallese are adept at using shells to make very unusual items. One such item is a beautiful picture frame, made by Steve Kellin, as a gift for our family, from him and Likyjon.

The wooden frame is decorated with tiny black and yellow snail shells in the form of a lovely palm tree, topped with tiny white augers to form the palm frond. Different colored volute shells form a bunch of ripe coconuts. Flowers of white miters *(mitra chrysame)* decorate the side of the frame, while the base has three shell flowers of white and orange variegated miters *(mitra stictica)*. The base flowers resemble floating water lilies that one sees on the lakes and ponds of the midwestern United States in the spring.

Another beautiful shell craft produced by the Marshallese is an all shell vase made of money cowries *(cypraea moneta L)*.

Palau District

The Palau District lies at the extreme western boundary of the Trust Territory of the Pacific, Micronesia. Located in the Western Caroline Islands, it includes the Palau chain which is about twenty-five miles wide by 125-miles long. There are four tiny isolated coral islands—Pulo Anna, Merrir, Sonsorol, and Tobi—lying to the southwest, and including the atoll of Helen Reef. In all there are only 185 square miles of land in the entire Palau District. Babelthuap, twenty-seven miles long by four to eight miles wide, is Palau's largest single land mass.

Palau has a boat-building industry and a commerical fishing industry. Much handicraft is produced on Palau. Palau's Van Camp fishing industry catches approximately 16,000,000 pounds of skipjack tuna a year. The Palauan coconut mill is capable of handling about 140 tons of copra per day. Its tourist industry is increasing yearly. Visitors from

Japan and many other places visit the Western Pacific in larger number each year.

Storyboards from Palau
Western Caroline Islands

Any visit to Micronesia is incomplete without the acquisition of a storyboard from Palau in the Western Caroline Islands. The long distances involved in transportation and the scarcity of these storyboards make this difficult. Many of the prospective collectors are serving tours of duty on Kwajalein in the Marshall Islands or on Guam in the Mariannas. The storyboards are carved or painted in Palau and air-freighted to Guam and Kwajalein, spasmodically, distances of twelve hundred and twenty-four hundred miles respectively.

Today's most prized storyboards are carved in natural dort wood, a hard mahogany type wood. Originally, all the boards were painted. These are still produced today, but with commerical paint, which tends to lessen their value. The primitive originals were done in soft hues of traditional colors, made by the Palauans using soot, yellows and reds from ochre, and earth clay, and the lime from burned coral. Native artists learned to make paint by mixing these ingredients with oil extracted from the para oil nut.

The Palauan storyboards originated from the painted rafters of the bai, the community house, sometimes referred to as the "men's house." Before Micronesians learned to write in the European style, it was common practice to paint picture stories on the rafters telling of folklore and local happenings of community interest on such subjects as love, sex, and war.

The first storyboards to find their way into the Western World were rafters taken from a deteriorating Palauan bai by the Germans for their homeland museums. Germany obtained Micronesia from Spain in 1898 and administered the area until the advent of World War I, when the Japanese took over its administration. Later, Japan won a mandate from the League of Nations to continue its rule. Because bai do not deteriorate rapidly and as it would be tragic to destroy one of the storyboard rafters, this type of board became quite scarce.

The production of portable storyboards, as we know them today, began during the Japanese administration of the Marshall, Caroline, and Mariana Islands, which make up Micronesia. They initiated a handicraft project led by a Japanese artist and folklorist, Mr. H. Hijikata. He believed that the young Palauans, under his tutelege, would not only learn to paint and carve portable storyboards for commerical purposes but that they could gain a new insight into their own early folklore and Palauan mythology. When he left Palau, he had trained about a dozen new carvers and artists to make portable storyboards. He also re-instituted the art of producing Palauan statuary in wood. A strict traditionalist, he refused to grant his trainees permission to use any colors or paints other than the kind used on the original rafters. Hijikata believed that his pupils should adhere to the local style of art that they had learned by reproducing bai rafter paintings. He experimented, though, with natural wood carving, using traditional stories and myths, thus creating a new art form of the storyboard. Finding this a pleasing new medium, he proceeded to instruct his students in the new craft. One young Palauan student, named O'Siik, was especially talented. Today, the most prized and sought after storyboard carvings are those done in three dimensions on natural dort wood by the late O'siik's trainees. A finish coat of brown wax shoe polish waterproofs the work and gives it a lustrous sheen.

Following World War II, the United States received a Strategic Trusteeship from the United Nations to administer the Trust Territory of the Pacific, Micronesia. The first manager of the Palauan Island Trading Company, Mr. Taggart, rediscovered the craft of storyboard painting and carving. Storyboards are Palau's major contribution to the Western Pacific modern primitive art. Most of these are produced by Mr. Hijikata's former students and their own pupils.

One sees a vast stylistic difference in each individual carver's interpretation, as he carves and sketches an age old design on a board. The artist who is privileged to paint a new

40

bai rafter has an even greater freedom of expression because of the great size. The portable storyboards, of necessity, remain limited in size. They range from six inches to six feet in length and from four to twelve inches in breadth. Any unattached piece of wood, old or new, is utilized because of the scarcity of wood in the area.

To make a painted board, the artist first etches the outline of the story in the wood with a sharp instrument, then paints it. Today's use of prepared enamels shows the modern influence on the craft. The craftsmen no longer take the time to mix their own soft primitive colors. Enamel gives a garish harsh effect that is not nearly so pleasing to the eye as the traditional paints. Carved boards are made by hand with sharp knives, picks, or whatever tool is at hand. These tools would appear quite primitive by our standards. The artist sometimes carves his name deeply into the back of a finished board to sign his work. Each one has his own border, which he uses to identify his boards, after he becomes proficient in the art. Some students copy their master's border while they are studying. It takes some practice to recognize an unsigned board's artist. After working with many storyboards we learned to spot an O'Siik immediately. He was probably the master carver of Palauan storyboards.

The Fish Bearing Tree of Ngiptal Island
A Legend

Centuries ago on an island named Ngiptal, near the village of Ngial, lived an old woman, all alone on the shore. She bore a son named Mengidabrutkoil, but she seldom knew where he was or what he was doing, as he loved to travel to other villages, never taking care of his mother's needs.

The Ngiptalese passed the old woman's thatched hut daily returning from the sea with their fish. No one offered her any of their catch, so she was hungry most of the time.

After a long absence, Mengidabrutkoil came home to visit his mother one day. She complained to him that while the people in the nearby village of Ngial had plenty of fish to eat, she never had any for her pot. Her son listened dutifully to her complaint, then, before setting out on his next trip he went out into the yard and chopped a large branch off of the breadfruit tree with his sharp machete. As the branch fell to the ground, waster gushed through the hole, flowing spasmodically to the rhythm of the waves along the shore. With each surge, a fish hurtled through the gaping fissure and landed in the cooking pot, placed strategically beneath.

The tree became the envy of all the people on the island. "While we must daily go out to sea and toil for our fish, the old woman can get all the fish she wishes by just sitting under her breadfruit tree," was the general complaint. Finally, an envious old man, who could no longer bear his neighbor's good fortune, chopped down the fish bearing tree in the middle of the night. The water that had flowed forth intermittently through the hole, now burst upward in torrents, flooding the entire island. To this day, the sunken island, with its paved roadways and courtyards, can be seen shimmering beneath the water as you pass by in a canoe, off the shore of Ngiptal. There are many versions of this legend so two are given here.

Magic Breadfruit Tree LEGEND II

This is the breadfruit story of the island of Ngibtal near Ngiwal. In this story the female demigod Dirrachedebsungel, after having taught the people of Palau how to grow taro, settled down at Ngibtal as an old woman and was rewarded by the gods, who gave her a magical breadfruit tree with a hollow trunk and a broken limb. Up through this tree, with each wave, were driven quantities of fish which landed in Dirrachedebsungel's front yard. The villagers on the island finally grew jealous of the woman and her constant supply of fish, so a group of men cut the tree down, perhaps hoping to gain an abundance of fish for themselves. Actually, however, the ocean came up through the hollow stump and flooded the entire island. All the islanders except Dirrachedebsungel were drowned and she eventually went on, with the name

Milad, to give birth to four children who founded the villages of Melekeiok, Koror, Ngeremlengui, and Aimeliik.

The Palauan Bai
To Accompany Palauan Storyboards

The Palauan bai is a long sloped-roofed structure which has served several functions in the Palauan community. While no contemporary community would be without at least one bai, it was not uncommon for a single village to have four or five in the days prior to Western contact.

The Micronesian bai is described at length in a later story, so only the Palauan bai will be dealt with here.

15.

The bai of Palau are unique in that they are decorated frequently with the picture of a girl named Dilukai, a character from an ancient legend. Also they are covered with folklore in the form of paintings on the rafters of Palauan bai, known far and wide. From the bai rafters come the stories and legends handed down through the centuries for the present day portable storyboards. A favorite storyboard is a carving or painting of the bai (abai), known for centuries as the men's house or club.

Tekeok—Imid, the Woman Who Violated Custom
A Legend

In the Koror hamlet of Ngeremid stands a stone image which, according to anthropologists familiar with Oceanic artifacts, represents a fertility symbol in the form of a crocodile embracing a young woman. The local villagers tell a different story about the image, which, they insist, is a young mother holding her infant in her arms.

In Ngermid it was prohibited for a woman having just completed her bath in sea water to look upon the ruk, a male dance. Once when the men of the village were dancing, a young mother carrying her baby came over the mountain from Ngerieleb to watch. Because the woman had just completed bathing in the lagoon before she left her village, she was in violation of the law of Ngeremid and, with her infant, was turned into stone. The stone, known as Tekeok-Imid, remains as a warning to those who contemplate the violation of custom.

The Brave Boy and the Serpent
A Legend

Aimeliik is a wide, beautiful place near the shore in Babelthaup Island, Palau. No one remembers when the first people came, but it was long ago. Children like to hear stories of strange things that happened there in the old days. Once, a huge serpent lived on the island. He used to eat some of the people, when he was hungry. The people tried to kill him, but they were not successful. Year after year, the serpent took some of them. They lived always in fear of this great animal.

One day, the chief said, "I must take you away from the village. You will have to give up your homes and good land forever. We will start life in a new part of Babelthaup, far from Aimeliik." That was hard for the people to do, but they agreed to go. Soon there was great excitement. The people packed up their things and got into canoes. Would there be canoes enough for all? They were loaded very high. Many parcels had to be thrown out at the last moment. Even the chief had to leave some things behind.

A poor young woman went from canoe to canoe with her simple belongings. She tried to find a place, but no one made room for her. "Find someone else to take you," they all said. One by one the canoes sailed over the lagoon. When the last one departed, she was left behind on shore. She stood crying. Finally, she went back to the village, but she was afraid to stay there, for the serpent knew that place well. She took the things she needed and walked far up the mountains to a hidden valley. There she built a small hut for herself out of leaves.

In the daytime she hid herself in the dark hut. At night she went out and hunted for food. She never made a fire for cooking. If the serpent saw smoke above the trees, he would know that someone was there. She always ate her food uncooked. She lived in that way for some time. Then a baby boy was born to her, and she was very happy to have him. He grew fast, and was strong and clever. She watched over him day and night and kept him from going near the serpent. One day, when the boy was ten years old, he asked his mother why they lived without any people around them. She told him the story of the large serpent and showed him the village of Aimeliik, down by the shore, and told him why they could never make a fire.

The boy wanted to obey his mother, but from that time he thought about killing the serpent. Finally, he had an idea. He gathered together large bundles of dry firewood, and piled them upon the edge of a cliff on the mountainside. Day after day he worked from early morning until night. He also gathered large rocks and dragged them to the cliff. It was hard work for a young boy, but at last there was a large pile of wood and rocks. He then asked his mother to show him how to build a great fire. His mother was frightened and she cried, "What a poor son you are. You want to build a fire? I have told you why we must never do such a thing. If the serpent sees the smoke of even a small fire, we won't live much longer." "I am quite ready to meet the serpent," replied the boy. "Let me have a fire."

Finally, she consented. They rubbed dry sticks together to get a spark, and let it ignite the dry coconut husks. Soon, there were flames enough to burn the wood. The smoke went higher and higher in the sky. The serpent was hungry, and he saw smoke in the valley, so he went there. He was so large and strong that as he moved along, thick breadfruit trees and tall coconut palms fell crashing down. The poor mother saw the serpent, and she ran around her poor little leaf hut crying. She felt sure that the serpent would take her boy and then come and get her. The boy, however, calmly stood beside the pile of stones and held a long pole and tended the fire. The stones became hotter and hotter. "Let the serpent come, I am ready for him," he said. The serpent came into the valley and crawled up to the cliff. His eyes shone like fire, and he opened his ugly mouth in anticipation of his meal. Quickly the boy pushed hot stones into it, working fast with his long pole. The serpent did not want to swallow hot stone, but he swallowed a great many of them before he knew what was happening. By then it was too late to stop; and by that time he could no longer close his mouth. Soon he rolled over and died.

The boy's mother came running to him. "My brave son, you have killed the serpent," she said. The boy cut open the serpent's belly and took out the bladder. He put it in a wooden dish which once had belonged to the chief of Aimeliik. Then he carried the dish down to the lagoon and put it in the water. Before it floated away, he spoke to it, saying, "When you reach the place where the chief and his people now live, they will ask you questions. Remain just as you are, until they ask you if you are part of the serpent of Aimeliik. Then swell up very large."

The dish floated away on the tide. In a few days it came to the place where the people lived, in a new village named Ngebuked. They all came running to see the strange thing. The chief looked at the wooden dish and the bladder and knew that the dish had once been his own. He asked many questions of it. Nothing happened. Then he asked if it was part of the serpent of Aimellik, and the bladder began to swell, and it continued to swell more and more, until it was as large as a basket. The chief knew then that the serpent had been killed.

"Now we can go home to Aimeliik," he said. The people were glad. They ran to pack up their things. They got the canoes ready, and in a few days they sailed back to their old home. They boy was ready for them. He made some sharp spears and waited at the shore. He was angry with the people for what they had done to his mother. The canoes crossed the lagoon, but the boy would not let them come near the shore. "You have no right to come here," he shouted. "Stay back or there will be a big battle; I can tell you, I will fight all of you!" The chief and his people had nothing to fight with, but they wanted to come back to their home without any trouble. "Never," shouted the boy. "You have no land in Aimeliik now. Just remember that my mother was left here alone when the rest of you went away. I intend to make you pay for it." "We did wrong. We will never do anything like that again," said the people. But the boy raised his spears still higher. Finally, the chief said, "You are a brave boy. We will give you whatever you ask if you will let us stay." The boy thought it over. "Very well, then," he said, "I will take half of the land for my mother and myself. The rest of you may share the other half. But don't forget—the poor people of our village must always be helped. That must be a rule in Aimeliik from this time on."

Everyone agreed, and the people all settled in Aimeliik. The boy became a rich man and a leader. His mother was happy, and the pile of stones is still on the mountain where the brave boy must have put them long ago.

The Story of Tebang
A Legend

Once a man from Ngiwal, named Rekesiwall, went to Ngerngesang hamlet, in Ngchesar, and there married a woman named Merderad, and settled down. By Merderad he had a son named Tebang; but while Tebang was still an infant Merderad died. Rekesiwall lived on in the hamlet, devoting his life to raising his son.

Years later, when he had reached maturity, Tebang married a girl from Ngerengesang. But with his marriage, Tebang's affection for his father steadily decreased until at last he ordered Rekesiwall out of the house. Rekesiwall returned sadly to his native village of Ngiwal, only to find his home gone and all his relatives dead. He was too old now to build a house or go out fishing, and was forced to live in the village abai and beg people for food.

Back in the village of Ngerngesang, Tebang went one day into the forest with his friends to fell a tree for a canoe. After hewing the timber roughly into shape, they dragged it towards the sea. On the way, however, it slid into a taro patch and, despite all their efforts, Tebang and his friends could not drag it out. They tried again with the help of the sixty men of the village, but the canoe still remained stuck in the taro patch.

They decided to take their problem to a diviner. He took a coconut, cracked it open and after examining the edge where the shell had split, announced that the mishap was punishment for Tebang's failure to look after his father. Tebang immediately got into a canoe and sailed to Ngiwal where he found Rekesiwall in the abai. He told his father he was sorry for having neglected him for so many years. "Come and live with us in my home from now on, and we shall share with you whatever fortune befalls us."

So Rekesiwal returned to Ngerngesang with Tebang and supervised the hauling of his son's canoe from the taro patch. While he chanted, the men strained at the towing in time to his rhythms, and the canoe was dragged all the way to the beach. Ever after that, Rekesiwall lived happily in his son's home.

48

The Story of Yap Stone Money
A Legend

The value of the massive rai, or stone money of Yap, dates back many centuries to the time when a fishing canoe from Balabat, Rul, was driven 250 miles southwest of Yap by a tropical storm and forced to land on an uninhabited portion of Palau. While the crew of the canoe were resting and regaining their strength, one of them found a large piece of limestone similar in shape to a whale. The man who found the stone felt that it would be good luck for the survivors to take the whale-shaped stone back to Yap as a gift to their king, rather than the traditional gift of fish. When they reached Yap once again, the crew went to the king and gave him the stone that had been found in Palau. They told the king that they had almost lost their lives while catching fish for him, and therefore the stone fish should be acceptable to the king, and considered as even more valuable than other Yapese treasures.

The king was happy to see the return of his subjects from , it seemed, the dead, and was very proud of the gift they had brought to him. He had the stone whale put into his treasury, and as the story spread over Yap, it gained in prestige and value, both because of its rarity and because of the danger and adventure that had accompanied its acquisition. Soon teams of Yapese were making the long trip to Palau to quarry the limestone.

At first the shape in which it was quarried was left up to the workers, but gradually the round shape evolved as the best, and the hole in the center was put there to pass a log through so the stone piece could be more easily carried. It is reported that the discus shape of the rai was developed by a man from Rul Municipality on Yap, proper, and a man from Ulithi, an atoll about one-hundred miles northeast of Yap. The word rai is the name given the stone money by part of Yap, as well as Tamil, Gail, Map, and Rumung. The rest of Yap calls it fee, which is Ulithian in origin. The word rai means, literally, whale, and refers back to the original piece of limestone brought to the king on Yap.

Most of the stone money was quarried at Babelthuap in

Palau District. A few pieces were taken from Guam, and these are the most valuable. At a later date, limestone was found in Talangith, a village in the northern part of Yap. However, no value is placed on the money quarried there because no toil was expended in transporting it. Today there is one remaining piece of Talangith rai in Teb, Tamil. The Yapese call it daniyor, which means literally, no tears— because nobody wept when the quarriers went to dig out the stone discs as they did when teams departed for Palau or Guam. The relatives of those who went far away to quarry stone money had reason to weep because the teams remained away for as long as three years. And in this region of tropical storm, many teams with their treasure of rai were lost at sea.

During Japanese times on Yap, stone money, quarried in Guam, which was a foot in diameter, was worth the equivalent of seventy-five dollars in Japanese currency. Palau discs, three feet in diameter, were worth twenty-five dollars per foot of diameter. The value of the stone money depends upon its history as well as upon its size, quality, color, shape, and age. With the decline in Yapese population from more than 40,000 to 42,000, the histories which were passed down by word of mouth from generation to generation have mostly been lost.

Prior to contact with European and American traders and whaling ships in the mid-nineteenth century, parties of as many as fifty men would sail off on quarrying expeditions. The rai would be returned to Yap in canoes or on rafts. However, with the coming of foreign ships, the larger pieces were often transported in foreign schooners, including the schooner owned by the legendary American trader, O'Keefe. Quarrying and importing rai continued through the early days of Japanese occupation. The larger rai weigh several tons. However, transactions involving the larger pieces do not necessarily involve transportation. Title to a piece of stone money is transfered, and the exchange is made public, but the stone may remain where it is. A survey made by the Japanese in 1929 found 13,281 pieces of stone money. There isn't a public report available now, but it is believed that about fifty percent of the stone money was destroyed during World War II.

16.

Royal Palauan Money

There are several versions of the discovery of Palauan money. In one, a boy and his father, discover a new island, Ngerot Island, which is covered with small, strange looking stones. After collecting several and taking them back in the canoe, they find that the stones are royal Palauan money. Royal money, depicted here, is of red stone, or coral, quite hard with a white marbled effect in the stone. It is cut and shaped to fit the neck and threaded with a piece of woven cord. Brides wear this money as a part of their dowry for the wedding, and continue to wear it thereafter. Some is cut into oval shapes, and attached to chains by today's artisans.

Black Coral
Trees by Polynesians
Jewelry from Palau

Deep down in the sea, growing out of the coral reef in the lovely blue lagoons, scuba divers have found a graceful white seaweed. This is attached with tenacity to the coral reef, gently swaying with the water's motion. Under that deceptive white covering grows the exquisite black coral.

Obak, of Palau, is a designer and carver of fine jewelry from the black coral. One piece, a necklace, is made of slender one-inch pieces of the black coral and attached to each other with gold or silver jewelry chain links. He adds a round pendant made of black oyster to the center of the necklace, giving it an elegance that makes its recipient the envy of all who see it. Copper wire, instead of gold, is frequently used, as it is more easily available.

Hawaiians, who live and work in the Marshalls, are masters at forming perfectly shaped trees from the black coral. Because this craft is performed by Polynesians in the Marshall Islands of Micronesia, and because these creations are highly prized by anyone receiving one, it deserves a place in the *Micronesian Handicraft Book.* The artisan removes the white lime deposit from the coral by soaking it in warm sea water, thus leaving the shiny black coral ready to shape or carve into jewelry or trees.

Coral found growing on the side of the coral reefs of Micronesia grow at a depth of sixty feet or less. At much deeper depths, divers may find the fragile Hawaiian coral in Micronesia, as in Polynesia. Its feathery branches are very thin and indescribably beautiful.

Dilukai—Palauan Statuary

Dilukai is the name given to all Palauan statuary. The exact reason for this Palauan word's use for all their statuary is unknown. It is believed, though, that the most prominent early primitive statue was a girl called Dilukai. Her likeness was painted on all early bai. Today, she adorns many model bai that are carved for the handicraft market. The following legend is associated with Dilukai.

17.

The Legend of Dilukai

Dilukai was an errant sister to a hard-working, hot tempered Palauan man. In Palauan society, there is no closer economic relationship than that between a sister and brother. Socially, they may appear distant, but in fact the brother-sister link is the strongest in the chain of economic

53

18.

exchanges, so typical of Palauan culture.

Dilukai was an exception, however. She was lazy. She teased her brother when he was trying to do serious, productive work and she irritated him so much that eventually he could stand it no longer. In a fit of rage, he grabbed a coconut-husking stick and took after Dilukai through the jungle. Fortunately, Dilukai was swift of foot. She arrived, well ahead of her brother, at a place where several men were in the process of constructing a bai. She asked the men for help. They suggested she jump up on the uncompleted gable above the door of the bai and hold her grass skirt well above her waist when her brother arrived. This she did, performing the worst possible insult that a female can, and her brother, shocked, left the scene never to be heard of again (in this version of the story).

Dilukai properly appears naked on the Palauan club bai (no images are currently in existence) and is supposed to symbolize the horror of bad relationships between brother and sister. Other sources, however, suggest that Dilukai was simply a famous instance of a girl companion living in a male bai and that this common practice received commemoration through her statue on the club bai.

Micronesian Bai

On many islands in Micronesia, there is a community house, called a bai. While visiting a Protestant church on an island in the (Madolenihmw) District of Ponape, in the Eastern Caroline Islands, we were privileged to see and take pictures of their unusual bai. All bai (abai) differ in construction. Seldom, are two built identically. The Madolenihmw bai was large, a sixty-by-eighty-foot Polynesian-type abode thrusting its peaked thatched roof sixty feet into the air from the dirt floor. This bai, beautiful still, though old and deteriorating, was constructed of a thatched roof attached to structural timbers. Woven coconut fiber mats, strategically placed to leave spaces for doors and low openings for ventilation, formed the sides. Several families of the Madolenihmw tribe, from all over the district, were gathered that day to await the death of their nanmwarki (king), who was hospitalized nearby in a modern Western infirmary.

Visiting families were using the age-old bai as a hotel. Here they planned to remain, carrying out their daily living functions, until the death and funeral of the dying nanmwarki. The coronation of the new king would immediately follow the Christian funeral service.

Inside this bai, many overhanging balconies were built in tiers. Each level was assigned as sleeping quarters to families, according to the status of the family head. Thus, the highest ranking chief received the top tier, with the lowliest finding space on the dirt floor. Few bai have dirt floors anymore. Elevated floors on posts are the contemporary vogue. An elevated floor will keep dry better during the rainy season and provides a cleaner working and resting surface. It also provides a good ventilation system utilizing the cool breezes by allowing them to flow through it. Most do not have tiers for communal living so it was a treat to see the Madolenihmw fully occupied.

Another unique feature of this bai was the location of the cooking ohms in the dirt floor inside the doorway. The ohms, holes dug in the dirt, measure about three feet in diameter and are eighteen inches deep. They are filled with coral and cooking wood, and the cooking pots placed above. These are normally housed in a separate thatched hut. This enables the cooks to keep the cooking clutter out of the living area. Here, the cooking, laundry (done by hand in modern plastic tubs), plus the tending of the children, were all being carried out around the ohm inside the bai. As the pots bubbled with rice steaming in coconut milk, the women scrubbed clothing. Children played quietly nearby. Several pigs and chickens ran loose around the fires, rooting and scratching—enjoying their last days of freedom. They were scheduled for the cooking pots of the coronation feast.

Elsewhere in the Territory, bai are also built of structural timber and covered with thatched roofs. The sides are of woven coconut fiber mats, with the buildings being much smaller than at Madolenihmw. On Palau, wooden rafters are attached to the structural timbers. Deeply carved and painted with stories and legends, these rafters depict the Palauan chronicles of many generations in pictographic permanence.

Prior to Western contact, some villages contained as many as four bai. Early bai functioned as men's meeting places and dormitories. Later, men formed clubs for both single and married fellows, using the bai as their center. Village councils were held in some bai. Public works were discussed, including the building and repairing of the canoe fleets so vital for fishing and transportation. They decided how to divide the daily catch and who would fish. The weaving of nets and sails was accomplished in the bai. While the council met, men worked at the weaving. During food shortages, they sometimes decided how to divide the food—coconuts, pandanus fruit, taro, breadfruit, oranges, limes, whatever they had to divide—at the bai. Other issues discussed were the amount of taro and copra to harvest.

This village center also served occasionally as a military and security headquarters. The men rallied there to provide protection against hostile warriors from other tribes, who might try to invade the island by canoe. Often they protected the whole village from foreign whaler crews, who loved to plunder, rape and destroy the culture of these primitive people for fun and profit. In the club-bai system, the men were often furnished female companionship from a nearby village. Local women were never allowed in the bai, but were sometimes called on to serve in other villages. During the German administration of the region, the club-bai ceased to exist, outlawed because some of its activities were considered immoral.

Today's bai serves many functions in an island community, and is used differently on every island, it seems. On some outer islands, the bai is constructed near the dock to serve as a guest house for off-island visitors. During the day it is a favorite gathering place for the village elders. Here they can visit, hail passing canoes for news, weave fishing nets, carve and weave handicraft, and snooze. They enjoy playing a special checker game with pieces of coral on a board carved on the raised floor. They are in a prime location to receive their share of the day's fishing bounty when the fishing fleet returns.

All over the rapidly Westernizing Trust Territory, today's bai serve both men and women as community centers. Civic leaders call meetings to discuss educational needs, hold political elections, gather for celebrations (Christmas and other holidays), work out solutions to food shortages and other items of current local concern. However, with most islands now having one or more school buildings, the bai begins to lose its prominence as the central meeting place. Still, each bai emits an unfathomable charm as it weds yesterday's primitive Micronesian culture with the Westernizing influence of today's schools, organized government, and dollar economy, into tomorrow's heterogeneous culture.

Palauan Illengel

The Palauan vase, or illengel, was originally a large carved wooden container made to hold a fermented coconut beverage used on all the Islands. This drink is known in the Marshall Islands as jacaroo or jemanon.

19.

Today, large illengels are rarely made, but miniatures are produced for a variety of uses, such as vases, pencil holders, ashtrays, and as lovely wooden carvings for collectors. Some have been made into modern articles, such as pepper mills and table lighters. Others are deeply carved story cups, with legends carved thereon.

It was a real delight for our family to finally obtain a large illengel, after waiting for two years. Looking at the age-old carved figures, we were amazed to see that the Palauans had carved an airplane as one of their sculpted pictures. This is a wonderful example of the incorporating of modern objects into today's crafts, wedding the new with the traditional and ancient.

Medechiibelau and Itungelbai
A Legend

This is the story of two gods, Medechiibelau of Airai, and Itungelbai of Aimeliik. These two gods were very good friends. One day, Medchiibelau went to visit Itungelbai, finding him tending his huge school of mechas, a small, delicious lagoon fish. Medechiibelau asked his good friend if he would permit him to herd the fish one time around the island of Babelthaup, and Itungelbai gave his permission.

Medechiibelau, however, as soon as he had control of the fish, herded them quickly toward Airai. Upon realizing this, Itungelbai became angry and threw many kinds of sea shells and animals after Medechiibelau. These mostly landed in the water around Aarai, short of their mark.

This is the reason why, about three times a year, the mechas appear in large numbers off the coast of Airai. The people of Airai celebrate the occasion with a huge feast, inviting those of other hamlets to join in. Also, because of this incident, one can find a large abundance of sea shells and animals in the lagoons of Aimeliik.

Money Pot
Palau

For many years, long ago, Palauans used a money pot to store their money. There was, supposedly, a money pot in each household.

Today, Palau is on the dollar economy, so the Palauan seldom uses such a money pot. The money pot is still carved and inlaid with shells for the handicraft trade, however, and some are very ornate and beautiful.

Tobi Monkey Men
Western Caroline Islands

Tobi Island, in the Western Caroline Islands, near Papua and Indonesia, is more characteristically Melanesian than Micronesian.

For centuries, the Tobi people have carved wood statues resembling a monkey or ape. These were first discovered for the Western world by the Germans when they visited the islands in the late 1890s. The statues, ranging in size from two to twenty inches high, were used as house or ancestral gods, in much the same manner as a shrine is in a Japanese household. Others were carved to accompany a deceased person set adrift in a canoe for a traditional burial at sea. The latter use, as a companion or guardian to the spirit of the dead, was the most important function of the statue, and it may have been considered a "spirit god." Although the statues lost value as a myth spirit when the islanders were converted to Christianity, they gained monetary value to the carvers who used them for barter during the German administration. Recognized as a primitive art form, their value continued to increase, and during this century, they have gained popularity and value as a commerical handicraft.

The monkey men were called Tobi-ningyo (tobi-doll) by the Japanese when they administered the islands. By the

1930s, the statues had gained popular acclaim as a curio and were being imitated in Palau and Ulithi. Originally fashioned from a soft, heavy-grained wood (called baderirt in Palauan), the monkey men statues are usually made from the Palauan dort (ifel) wood today. Dort wood is comparable to American mahogany and is available to Tobi Islanders who have migrated to Palau and continue their carvings as a livelihood.

Western Caroline Islands
Yap District

Located about 450 miles southwest of Guam, Colonia is the administrative center for the Yap District. The inhabited islands stretch seven-hundred miles to Satawal. Yap is made up of four major islands, separated by narrow passages, fringing or barrier reefs. The eastern outer islands are low lying, with lagoons in atolls.

Yap, Ulithi, and Woleai all have inhabited islands.

The field trip boats visit the outer islands two to four times yearly, while Yap itself, is served by scheduled jets and the regularly scheduled ships going to and from Japan for food supplies for the Trust Territory, though these are sometimes two weeks late and other times early.

Copra and trochus shell are the main exports of Yap and most essential food is grown there.

Ulithi Monkey Men
Yap—Western Caroline Islands

Ulithi monkey men are carved from coconut or other soft wood. They are copied from the early Tobi monkey men, but are much larger with a distinctive style of their own.

Ranging in size from ten to twenty inches tall, they have a stocky torso and are almost squarish in appearance, somewhat resembling an owl.

20.

Model Yapese Money

The rai, or stone money, is famous all over the world for its massive size and adventuresome quarriers, dating back several centuries. The rai (meaning whale) refers to the first piece returned to the king of Yap. The rai is explained at length in the section devoted to storyboard.

Thick, round-shaped limestone was quarried. As stated previously the first money brought back to Yap was a whale-shaped piece that the crew of a storm-lost canoe found on Palau. They presented the whale stone money to the king. Soon, men were leaving to sail to Palau to quarry more stone money. Some was quarried as far away as Guam, and the distance increased its value. It was at great risk that the crew transported the money, by canoe, back to Yap. After quarrying a huge hole in the center of each piece, a pole was threaded through, enabling many men to carry it from the quarry to the canoe. The hole also made it lighter and easier to stabilize in the canoe.

Today, on Yap, small pieces are cut for the handicraft market. Old pieces are very valuable and are still owned and used for trade and barter on Yap.

Truk District

Stretching three-hundred miles wide by six-hundred miles long, the Truk District's one-hundred islands are scattered over 180,000 square miles of water area. Forty of the approximately one-hundred islands are inhabited, with Moen Island, in the Truk Atoll, serving as the administrative center.

Their principal exports are copra and cacoa. The Trukese fish and farm for their own food supply. Breadfruit, yams, fish, cooking bananas, tapioca, fresh fruit, rice, and taro—all are included in the Trukese diet.

There are two parochial high schools on Truk, Protestant and Catholic, and several public schools. The Mizpah High School, built in the 'sixties, a Protestant school, has been phased out. The many public schools, located throughout the Trust Territory, seem to be filling the demand for school space, thus enabling the church schools to get out of the business of teaching.

Mats and Baskets
Truk District

Each island group has its own unique style of weaving; such is true of the Central Caroline Islands group, the Truk District.

Many artifacts are made by the Fefan Women's Club and other clubs on the atoll. Pandanus or coconut fiber is woven around the coconut rib, which is split to the desired width, as on other island groups. Cut slightly wider though, the Trukese fiber strip has a sturdy appearance. Commerical dyes are not so widely used in the outlying Trukese Islands. Using carbon paper, for its purple dye, on the natural bleached fibers, the Trukese women painstakingly prepare strips from the coconut and pandanus fronds. These are used in the manufacture of baskets.

Their baskets have very intricately woven designs, which appear difficult to make and are very pretty. Some mats are decorated with tortoise shell centers, as are some of the baskets. Mats have coconut fringes, shell borders, or edges crocheted from pandanus or coconut fiber. The most unique baskets are those woven entirely of the fibers, in exquisite designs of flowers and lace. Narrow fiber strips are used to attach shell edgings, or to make fringe and crocheted trimmings.

Mortlock Devil Masks
Truk District

The devil masks of Mortlock are believed to be an art form of mask-making, which has been traced through Indonesia to the early Indian primitives. Some tracings go back to a late Chou tradition in China, around 600 B.C.

The masks are sometimes hung on canoe sheds and men's houses in Mortlock as spirit gods. An oldster recalled when the mask was used in dances to show the power of the spirit world.

Made either as female or male, the masks may range in size from six inches to six feet in height. The mask shows an elongated face with carved nose, painted eyes, with mouth turned up or down, depicting and depending upon the god's mood. Each has a high forehead with painted hair and hair ornaments, including a comb in the male's hair. The styles do not vary much, and the masks are painted black and white and adorned with a geometric border.

Trukese Love Stick

The most famous handicraft from Truk is the traditional love stick, with its charming legend, which has been passed down through the ages.

In the olden days, the love stick served as a nocturnal calling card for the young men of Truk. Carved by hand, each love stick is unique. Watching her favorite young man carve, a young girl would memorize his design.

As twilight faded, and courting time came to the island, a young man would push his carved love stick through the side of his favorite girl's grass hut. Because there were no lights, the girl had to rely on her memory of the carving, feeling the design of the love stick to determine its maker.

If the damsel approved of the calling card, she would pull the love stick through the hut wall and let the suitor enter. Otherwise, she would push the stick back through the wall and reject the young lover.

Model Gecko
Letter Opener

Truk artisans do not produce many carved artifacts. The gecko letter opener portrays the importance given to the tiny lizard. This animal has a strange effect on all new residents of the Trust Territory of the Pacific, until one becomes accustomed to it. I chased one around the counter-top with a broom, scooped it into the dust-pan and tossed it out the door, the day after my arrival in the islands for a rather lengthy stay. A man told me that I wouldn't see another gecko, as they had a grapevine communication, and that I would be deluged with moths and other insects for lack of them. True—for six months I never had a gecko return to the house, but I did have lots of moths around the outside lights. One night, we watched fascinated, as a gecko devoured moths while walking around on the outdoor ceiling of the overhang. The insects that he devoured, after having been away so long, were almost as large as the gecko. From then on, the gecko was our friend, and treated like one.

The gecko is a small lizard inhabiting warm climates, that has a short, flat body covered with tiny scales. Its unusual feet are composed of a toe pad with thousands of tiny hairs. These enable it to stick to flat surfaces in an upside down position, allowing access to the insects upon which it preys. It can walk well on rough areas with the aid of its tiny hidden claw.

The gecko letter opener, carved on Truk, depicts the long tongue of the tiny lizard, which pops out to grab its prey.

Lava Lava
Truk—Central Caroline Islands

On Truk, many men still wear some form of lava lava, a thu, or skirt. Most of today's men use cotton fabric, winding it around the waist and tucking it into a fold, thus draping it like a sarong. The lava lava, or thu, covers the loins and makes a short skirt-like garment. The men are usually bare from the waist up when they wear a lava lava.

The lava lava of yesterday was made of strips of bark or of a woven fiber, often pandanus, which was dyed and tightly woven into a long piece of material with a wide fringe. This fiber is soft to touch, but stiff to tie.

Eastern Caroline Islands
Ponape District

The volcanic peak of Sokehs is called the "Diamond Head of Micronesia." Ponape Island is the administrative center of the district, and with its high rainfall and lush green foliage, it is known as the "Garden of the Pacific." The Ponape District consists of two large volcanic islands, Ponape and Kosrae, and eight coral atolls. Ponape Island is the second largest in the Territory of the Pacific.

The district, with about eighteen thousand inhabitants, has an agricultural economy. Beans, pepper and rice are raised for cash crops. Much more rice could be raised on Ponape if the land were kept cleared, but this involves much work. Ponape pepper is exported to the United States and is of high quality. Cocoa is a new crop being tried.

Ponape District has a new airfield that is able to accommodate the 727 jet. Until the new field was completed, Ponape was serviced spasmodically by the SA 16, a sea-amphibian plane, and by field trip boats traveling to and from Japan.

Kapingamarangi Model Canoe

Kapingamarangi, a luxuriant palm covered coral island, is situated about one degree north of the equator in the Western Pacific Ocean, about three thousand miles southwest of Honolulu. Its inhabitants are of Polynesian descent. The women are quite beautiful, having an apricot colored skin, warm brown eyes, and long, flowing, silky, dark brown hair. They wear grass skirts and still adhere to the topless culture, as they have for centuries. The men are tall, bronze skinned, and handsome. On this island many men still wear thus (loincloths), or pandanus woven lava lava, the sarong skirt, tied on the side at the waist, described previously. Many wear lava lavas made of cloth, if available, as it is more pliable and comfortable to tie and to keep in place.

Many of these islanders migrate to Ponape, a distance of about four-hundred miles, six degrees north of the equator. There, they find homes in Kapingamarangi village with relatives or friends. They are able to earn money at handicraft carving and other jobs. Some attend the Pacific Islands High School, on Ponape, to prepare themselves to go back home as teachers or to go on to a higher education.

Each morning a fleet of sleek canoes, with white sails blowing in the sea breezes, leaves the dock at the foot of this enchanting thatched roofed village to fish for the day's catch.

The elders gather in the bai and weave their fishing nets, or carve model canoes and other handicraft. The model canoes are exact replicas of those used in the fishing fleet. They range in size from six to thirty-six inches in length by approximately two inches in width. Coconut fiber is woven for the model's sail. Made of coconut wood, the canoes are assembled with wooden dowels and have a miniature outrigger on one side, made to the proper scale.

The standard Kapingamarangi canoe is about eighteen-feet long and two-feet wide, with an outrigger on one side extending out to a distance equal to about one-half the length of the canoe. The sail is triangular, but the rigging is quite different from that of Western sailboats. In Micronesia, the sail is set so that as the boat changes its tack into the wind—first one end, and then the other, acts as the bow of the boat. Present day Kapingamarangi sailboats use canvas sails, instead of woven coconut or pandanus fiber, but the models adhere to the traditional native woven materials.

Model Fish, Canoe Bailer, Fishing Hook and Bait Box
Kapingamarangi Village

Everyone who goes out in a boat knows the wisdom of carrying a bailing bucket of some kind. The Kapingamarangi carvers make a bailer for use on all their canoes, and a tiny bailer is included in the model canoes as well. The bailer is bought as a handicraft item by collectors because of its hand carving and many decorative uses. Filled with Christmas balls of bright colors, it makes a lovely seasonal centerpiece. Holding wooden fruit from the Philippines, or artificial vegetables and fruit from the five-and-dime it makes a year round table decoration. Some people even use them for bailers!

Other artifacts are carved in the village. One is a finely detailed fish carved from coconut wood; a hook and a bait box for the fisherman are others, which also find their way into the collectors' hands.

Coconut Grater
Kapingamarangi Village

Kapingamarangi is inhabited by Polynesians and lies just barely north of the equator. Due to its location, it is far off the path of field trip boats, which call only a couple of times yearly.

The natives of Kapingamarangi like to migrate to Kolonia, several-hundred miles north, in Micronesia, where they have their own lovely thatched roof village. The entire village is constructed of thatched roof architecture with lovely paths, bordered by coleus, which grows in the tropical warmth to a height of several feet and is brilliantly colored. Here, they make many simple, but beautiful, pieces of handicraft that are really difficult to hack out of the hard wood available to them. They use an adz, a very primitive tool, to carve the coconut grater, which is made in many sizes. Some are as small as six-inches high; others range to as much as twenty-four inches. Teeth are carved in a piece of shell and tied with coconut rope to the carved neck of the wooden seat, thus making a bench coconut grater.

Green Coconut Leaf Tray
Ponape—Eastern Caroline Islands

The Ponapean women make a green coconut palm leaf basket that is really a shallow tray. Made on the same principle as are the green coconut leaf plates that they make and use daily all over Micronesia, they unwind the green palm leaf from the tree trunk before it unfurls.

The tender green leaf is cut, with a machete, into narrow strips. These strips are wound tightly around coconut ribs, which are then sewn together by hand to the desired shape—tray or basket. As the basket dries, after being finished, it becomes a soft, muted, grayish-green.

Ponape Dance Paddles, Spears
and
Love Sticks

All over Micronesia, the native men still participate in ceremonial dances for special occasions. Many local festivities are held, including a world holiday, United Nations Day, which is very important to all of the islanders.

At these celebrations many games are played, displaying skill and agility on the part of the contestant engaged in these very competitive sports. Basketweaving is demonstrated, while carving, rope-making and other skills are shown. Sometimes prizes are awarded to those being adjudged the best and a winner.

In Ponape, as in other island ceremonial dances, the men carry dance paddles, or spears, or clubs, the last usually made of lightweight wood comparable to our balsam. The Ponape dance paddle is black with white etchings and a white coconut fiber fringe. The women usually sit with their backs to the dancing men, and chant in rhythm for the men to dance; however, they do not watch.

A bulky spear-like love stick is carved in the Ponape

District. It follows the same legend as the Trukese love stick, which can be found in the Truk section.

The Ponape love stick is made of coconut or breadfruit and is large and bulky in appearance. Many spears are made of this heavy wood too, but usually these are not used for the dance.

Jar for Fermented Coconut Drink

There are two kinds of intoxicating beverages consumed in the Ponape District. One is Sakau, a fire-water made from pounding roots and pouring the pulp and juice together into a cup, which is passed first to the chief and then to everyone in turn. This is a very potent drink.

The other liquor is fermented coconut palm tree sap from the heart of the palm tree. Jars are strategically hung in the tree near the heart to catch the sap. This is a popular drink when it is available.

Tortoise Shell
Tortoise Jewelry

Frequently as you glide over the lagoon in a small sailboat or motorboat you pass very near a turtle or tortoise, which is large enough to overturn your small boat if it swims under just as you pass. The gleaming brown translucent shell with cream colored flecks make this creature's languorous strokes seem gracefully swift.

While visiting on Majuro once, I mentioned to Mary Lanwi that I hoped to get a tortoise to hang with the shells we had collected. That evening the albino turtle belonging to Dwight Heinie, the then District Administrator, disappeared. Since the administrator was Mary's brother, he knew of my request and teased me, saying that he hoped that Myrtle, his turtle, did not show up at the taxidermist. I was really relieved to leave Majuro without someone presenting me a stuffed turtle, for I feared I might be the recipient of Myrtle, Dwight's albino turtle!

A few weeks later, Myrtle came home, having been down on the Majuro beach, laying and burrowing her eggs. Shortly after that, Congressman Ekpap Silk came through by plane, on his way to Saipan to attend the new session of the Micronesian Congress. He brought the loveliest stuffed tortoise with a glossy mottled shell and left it with Cindy Silk, his cousin, to present to us. With Myrtle's safe return to her home, we joyfully accepted the lovely Majuro tortoise and proudly display it in our collection today.

The tortoise shell is used for many kinds of jewelry in Micronesia. The favorite from Ponape seems to be the rings made of tortoise and often trimmed with silver stars. The rumor is that the Micronesians use the fillings from their teeth to inlay silver into the rings and bracelets. Large pieces of tortoise shell are used in making fans and purses. Pendants, earrings and stick pins for hair ornaments are all carved from the decorative tortoise.

Grass Skirts and Neckbands
Ponape—Eastern Caroline Islands

Skirts in gaily colored, dyed tropical fiber are made by the dozens on Ponape from long coarse grasses. The top of the skirt is intricately woven in a finely spun design. Several layers of grass are combined to make a medium to heavy weight skirt that one cannot see through. Over the many layers of the finished grass skirt, the Carolinians crochet many beautiful designs of the grass fiber into an overskirt, which is then attached to the finished garment at the waistband. Each skirt seems to be original in design.

The skirts that are made in the Ponape District are more plentiful and colorful than the coconut fiber skirts of the Marshall Islands. This makes them less expensive and easier to obtain. The rarity of the coconut skirt makes it a treasured item, while the color and beauty of the grass fiber skirt entices the collector to want several of the coveted skirts to have many designs in trim for their collection.

The same technique of weaving is used to make fancy neckbands or waistbands like the Tahitians wear. The grass or coconut fiber is cut in twelve to fifteen-inch lengths and fashioned with a band at the top, then trimmed with crocheted pandanus fiber and shells.

Ivory Nut-Ponape

The islanders export the ivory nut today, but formerly they made charms and other articles from the ivory-like interior of the nut.

In James A. Michener's *Tales of the South Pacific*, a charm made from the nut is mentioned and described as, "one of the strange things of the islands."

When the ivory nut is completely dry, shell and nut, it rattles inside the husk when shaken by hand and is very heavy. Today the finest ivory buttons are made in Japan from ivory nuts imported from Ponape; these buttons are then exported around the world.

Ponape District Fans

Exquisite fans are made in the Ponape District. Attached to varied shapes and sizes of tortoise shell, pandanus fiber is woven around coconut ribs to form a border, of varying widths. Brightly colored chicken feathers interspersed with white provide a fancy finishing fringe.

The handles are covered with an intricately woven design in the pandanus fiber, much like the handles of the Marshallese fans.

Purses
Pingelap and Nukor
and
Other East Caroline Islands

All over Micronesia, where you find handicrafts being woven, you will find lovely handbags being made. Each island group makes its very own, distinctly different from other islands. On Pingelap, the handbags are made of the same materials as those found on other islands. The inside is woven of coconut fiber of natural color, while the outside is woven of natural coconut fiber interwoven with colorfully dyed fibers, making a gay and festive creation, which is often trimmed with dyed chicken feathers. Shells are fastened on the bottom of the bag to make little feet for the bag to rest upon, thus keeping it off of the coral. Because there is much humidity in Micronesia, this latter touch is much appreciated by the buyers.

The tortoise shell purses are made on Nukor and other Eastern Caroline Islands. They are unique and beautifully made of prepared pandanus fiber, which has been naturally bleached by the sun, then woven tightly around coconut ribs and fastened to large pieces of tortoise shell. The purses are woven into rectangular shapes measuring from six to ten inches by four inches. The woven rectangular top of fiber and shell completes the box-like purse of exquisite proportions and beauty.

Ponape Leis
Pandanus and Tangen Tangen Seed Pod

Many different kinds of fibers and seeds are used in making leis in the Ponape District. Probably the most popular is the pandanus fiber, which is dyed in many colors. Some leis are made in one color, while others combine two or more colors. Made of thickly gathered circlets which are securely fastened to hold their shape, the leis resemble those made of real flowers.

The tangen tangen seed pod is used in its natural color. Twisted into free form shapes or wound tightly into circles, it is threaded on string or wire alternately with seeds of Job's tears.

These leis can be worn with mu mus or other summer dresses, or the Islanders wear them with grass skirts.

Kosrae Dance Paddles
Eastern Caroline Islands

Kosrae, the second largest island in the Ponape District, is inhabited by friendly, but aggressively ambitious and hard-working dark-skinned people. It is the most peaceful and beautiful spot as you approach by ship and slip through the pass into its sleepy lagoon. Kosrae rises high out of the sea in volcanic peaks, which are covered with lush foliage of every imaginable green color and shade. The tangerines, oranges and limes grown there surpass any we have tasted elsewhere.

As there is no dock for large ships, they are forced to anchor out in the lagoon. Soon they are surrounded by canoes, some empty, to haul passengers by canoe to shore; others are filled with travelers laden with their luggage of woven green baskets, carrying a supply of pandanus, bananas, yams and breadfruit with lots of citrus to eat and for gifts. The Islanders usually travel as deck passengers to the other district centers, supplying their own sleeping mats and food enroute.

Colorful handicrafts are made on Kosrae. One of the prettiest is the dance paddle. This is carved in the shape desired, and then white etchings or carvings are made into the red-painted wood. Colored chicken feathers form a com-plimentary fringe.

Kosrae Fans
Eastern Caroline Islands

Fans made on Kosrae are of a utilitarian design. Closely woven pandanus, usually in somber colors or black and white, are made with covered woven handles. Well constructed and very useful, the fans from Kosrae are very unusual when compared to fans from other districts.

Mats and Baskets
Kosrae

Mats and baskets made by the Kosraens follow the same general principle as those of other districts; but, again a uniqueness stands out in the design and patterns.

Using thin strands of pandanus fiber, designs are crocheted into baskets and mats in delicate lacy patterns to form an exquisite creation in basketry.

In some mats, a heavier center design is made by winding pandanus fibers in various colors around coconut ribs and fastening the triangles, thus formed, together into a wheel or spiral center, which is then completed with a stiff serated coconut fiber fringe.

Seed Necklaces
Kosrae

Tangen tangen seeds are used in the handicrafts all over the Trust Territory of the Pacific. The necklaces made on Kosrae are not greatly different from other Micronesian necklaces. One sometimes sees elaborate designs formed of seeds fashioned into a necklace. Red jequirity and other tropical seeds are used with shells and tangen tangen seeds. Whatever their designs, they are always beautiful.

It is recommended, though, that a stronger thread be used for stringing by all Micronesians, who make necklaces. Stronger thread will assure greater wearability and longer durability for each strand.

Belt
Caroline Islands

The Caroline Islands outer Islands produce a brightly colored fiber belt, which is quite heavy in appearance. The belt is made of fiber and then decorated with many cowry shells. This belt resembles some of the American Indian weaving, but the Carolinian belt is made of the usual island fibers which makes it different, and instead of Indian beading, the Islanders use cowries. To make ties for the belt, coconut fiber is braided and attached with a fringed end to the finished belt. This makes a very attractive accessory to wear with summer cottons.

Mariana Islands
Marianas District

From Farallon de Pajaros to the north, extending three-hundred miles south to Guam, is the chain of Marianas.

There are 183 square miles of land in the district, including thirteen single islands and one group of three small islands. Guam is not a part of the Trust Territory. It is a possession of the United States.

Copra and agriculture and fish are all exported. Cattle are being experimentally raised on Tinian, and it is hoped to be able to supply much of the needed beef without the costly price of transporting it from New Zealand or the United States.

Saipan has served as the administrative headquarters of the

Trust Territory and is serviced by the 727 jet. There are several other aircraft in service between Guam and Saipan. Several new hotels have been constructed or are under construction plans for a growing tourist market.

On March 24th, 1976, Washington D.C. time, a seventeen-member Marianas delegation attended a ceremony at the White House and witnessed President Gerald Ford sign a resolution whereby the Mariana Islands became a Commonwealth of the United States. This enables the Marianas to have their own local government with a Commonwealth of Marianas Constitution, as they have citizen of the United States status.

A huge celebration on April 21, 1976 in Saipan was attended by Ambassador F. Hayden Williams, representing President Ford. Ambassador Williams brought a message from the President along with a copy of Public Law 94-241, which enacted the Covenant to Establish a Commonwealth of the Northern Mariana Islands in political union with the United States. The Covenant gives expression to the desire of the people for self-government within the American political system. The President added: "I extend my best wishes and congratulate you on your success in achieving the goal for which you have worked so hard. I share in your pleasure and welcome you as fellow Americans."

Shell Leis and Purses
Saipan—Mariana Islands

Marie Torres is an artist with shells. She crochets land snail shells into elegant leis, making earrings to match. The snails range in color from a soft yellow to medium brown with some of variegated stripes. She blends and mixes the colors for maximum effect into tastefully shaped purses and evening bags. Some are in envelope style, with a fold-over flap of the shells fastened with white chain crocheted strings to which stars of shells are attached. Others are made in cylindrical form, with the tops elaborately made of crocheted draw-strings fashioned with a bouquet of shells, which are tightly drawn to close the purse.

Their perfection and uniqueness defy description, and they must be seen to truly appreciate Mrs. Torres' great talent.

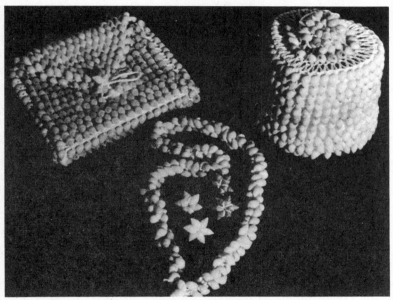

21.

Job's Tears Baskets
Saipan—Mariana Islands

The Tana Rosa Guild makes intricate baskets of Job's tears. So lacy and fragile looking are they, that you marvel at how they are able to hold their shape.

Job's tears seeds are strung on stiff copper wire and shaped into a diamond like pattern, as they are woven into several sizes and shapes of baskets.

Often they are shapely enough to be interwoven with pretty colored silk scarves and worn for a hat by anyone living in the islands who is lucky enough to obtain one. Others have handles and make lovely centerpieces when filled with wooden carved fruit from the Philippines, artificial fruit or jade fruit from the Orient. Real fruit makes an elegant centerpiece for a dinner party.

Tangen Tangen Seed Pod Wreaths
Saipan—Mariana Islands

Even the tangen tangen seed pod is dried and dyed; then it is turned into a work of art in wreaths for the holidays. These range in size from approximately two-inches thick to a diameter of twelve to twenty inches. The wreath can be used for door decoration. By filling the center with fresh fruit and nuts, one can create a sensational centerpiece.

The natural tan color of the tangen tangen seed pod makes an elegant wreath. However, rit dyes turn the pods lovely colors, and they make splendid handicrafts. The pod is divided and rolled inside out to form a loop and secured by wire or pins into a circular wire frame, forming a wreath.

Seed Curtains
Saipan—Mariana Islands

Several years ago, Dr. Wm. Vitterelli and his wife, Henrietta, were instrumental in aiding some Saipanese from two villages, San Rogue and Tanapag, to found a small handicraft business. The villages were extremely depressed economically, and Dr. Vit., as he is known by everyone, was anxious to help them to make handicrafts for export to Kwajalein and Guam. The fifty percent tariff on all Micronesian handicrafts exported to the United States makes it prohibitive. I trust the United States Congress will do something about removing this tariff very soon. To date, they have not. Dr. Vit., a Trust Territory staff member for twenty years, knew that the craft industry could provide a livelihood for many families. The Yukwe Yuk Club of Kwajalein operates a non-profit Micronesian handicraft shop in the air terminal with all volunteer help. All profits go into a scholarship fund for Micronesians. The shop committee advanced a thousand-dollar loan to the new Tana Rosa Company to enable it to begin making crafts for export.

Their first item was a seed curtain. Dozens and dozens of seed curtains were made by stringing one to two-inch lengths of bamboo, kukui seeds or nuts, and Job's tears to nylon fishing line. Each finished strand was attached to a twenty-eight to thirty-six inch heavy bamboo rod, at two-inch intervals. Swags were formed at the top of some curtains by draping several strands; others hung simply in long strands. The contrast of the gray Job's tears hanging with the large dark brown kukui seed and the beige bamboo makes an interesting and beautiful seed curtain. Each strand averages six feet in length. As with most Oriental or Oceanic crafts, each seed curtain is unique in design. Other handicrafts were made by Tana Rosa. Sales rose to hundreds of dollars on their crafts, and they soon repaid their loan with handicraft. I hope they are continuing and that business continues to grow yearly.

Necklaces and Belts
Saipan—Mariana Islands

Colored seed pods are tightly rolled from the tangen tangen plant and strung with brown tangen tangen seeds and Job's tears to form lovely leis and necklaces on Saipan.

The large dark brown kukui seed nut is strung on nylon fishing line with Job's tears and made into interesting belts.

Other crafts are made of the coconut shells and nuts and seeds that are not included in this book. This is a representative collection of all that is made in the Islands, but this book does not claim to describe a complete collection.

Seed Saw
Saipan—Mariana Islands

From seemingly useless scraps, the Saipanese fashion a balancing seed saw that is truly fascinating. A rounded end of a coconut shell is used for the base. To this is attached a medium sized piece of bamboo, about eight inches high and perhaps one-half inch thick. Atop the eight-inch bamboo they attach a balancing platform consisting of a one-and-one-half inch halved piece of bamboo with the hollow side facing up. A two-pronged twig, three inches long with the fork whittled to sharp points to serve as legs, is used, leaving one inch at the top for the body and neck of the balancing man. A kukui seed implanted with Job's tears for eyes and having a slit made for a mouth, is fastened to the bamboo neck. A tiny hold is drilled through the neck for an eighteen-inch, thin, green, and very pliable bamboo stick to be threaded. The thin bamboo ends are imbedded in large kukui seeds and bent to the proper degree to balance the man on the upturned hollow bamboo. This is a seed saw.

Saipanese Coconut Shell Doll
and
Seed Turtle

Everything is put to use in the Islands. Sea shells, the gemstones of Micronesian artifacts, are used in many crafts. Coconut shells from one of their staple foods are also left over from their most valuable export, coconut copra. The copra provides almost all of the income for outer Islanders, those living on islands away from the district centers. Nuts, fibers and seeds are used for making many articles, both for the Islanders' own use and for fashioning salable handicrafts.

From a halved coconut shell used for a neck, and a whole coconut shell serving as a head, a craftsman fashions a doll. Features are carved or painted on for a face, and a tiny kukui seed is implanted for a button nose. Often tiny shells are applied for ears to provide the finishing touch for the Saipanese Coconut doll.

A tiny turtle is evolved by using a large kukui seed nut as a body, to which four tiny elongated flower seeds are attached for legs. A large tropical bean implanted with a tiny bamboo piece forms the head and neck. Jequirity seeds are used for the eyes, as a tiny replica of the sea tortoise is produced in model form.

Bo Jo Bo Wishing Doll
Legend and Doll by Tana Rosa Guild

"My name is Bo Jo Bo. I come from San Roque, a little village in Saipan, Mariana Islands. I've been around a long time hiding in the woods and peeping out from the Bo Jo Bo vines. I am lovable, rich and strong. If you need some of my strength, love or money, you can have all I've got, but you must fold my arms for strength, cross my legs for love, and if you need money, tie my hands behind my back. Then all you need to do is hang me up where you can see me and have faith.

Remember my love comes from the seeds of my eyes, my wealth from the coconut fiber of my arms and legs and my strength from my Bo Jo Bo Nuts."

Glossary

Micronesian Word	Definition
abai or bai	men's house or community house
adz	ax
alu	small shell head band
baderirt	Palauan soft wood
belin	head lei
bit	pillow case of pillow cover
dilukai	Palauan statuary
dniyor	no tears
ejols	commoner
illengel	vase
iroij	king
ifel	dort wood
jacaroo-jemanen	fermented coconut drink
jamoa	loose fitting dress
jat	stick chart
jika or jikarej kej	cigarette case
kannir	belt
kano	table mat
kenwa	neck lei
kini or kinien	sleeping mat
kwo kannuij emmol	thank you very much
lava lava	fiber or cloth wrap-around skirt
likajjir	lei
nien mani	purse
nitijela	parliament
nanmwarki	king or highest chief
nuk-nuk	Marshallese dress
rai-fee	whale—Yapese stone money
sakau	potent root (ground) beverage
yukwe yuk	Marshallese greeting

22. Kili bag created by Bikini Islanders.

23. Marshallese Iroij sleeping mat—a gift from Dr. and Mrs. Isaac Lanwi.

24. Assortment of fancy Micronesian coconut and pandanus fiber mats.

25. Utilitarian green coconut leaf basket.

26. Unique fancy basket attached to its own mat—purchased by Greg Majuro.

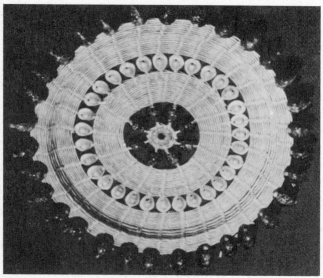

27. *Cypraea Caputserpentis* L. (brownie-snakeshead)—decorated baske gift from the Majuro Women's Clubs.

28. *Cypraea Moneta* L. (money cowries) give this basket from Arno Atoll its rare beauty.

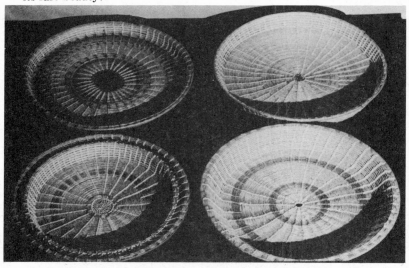

29. Fancy Marshallese baskets from Jaluit, Arno, Ailinglapa lap, and Majuro Atolls.

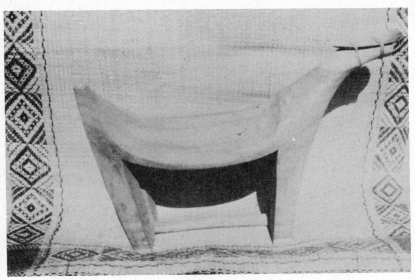

30. Caroline Islands coconut grater.

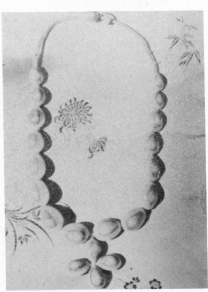

31. *Cypraea annulus* (L) (goldringer cowry) necklace—Marshallese jewels of the sea.

32. Marshallese belts—shells and fiber.

33. Coconut male and female doll from Ebeye—made by Wanjur.

34. Sea snail flower bouquet attached to a *Cypraea Tigris* (tiger) cowry, on left, shell corsage.

35. Alu shell head leis—Belin or Likajjir.

91

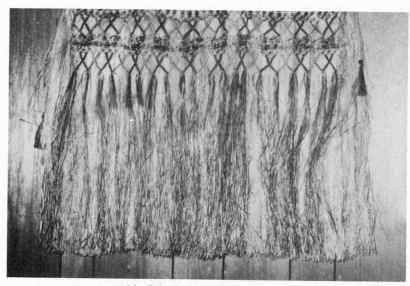

36. Caroline Islands grass skirt.

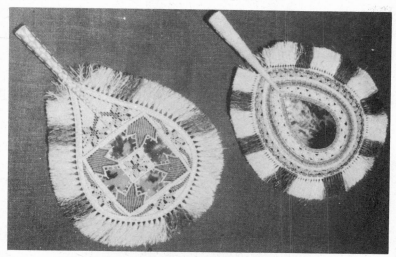

37. Marshallese fans, tortoise, coconut, and pandanus.

38. Left, Eastern Caroline fan, tortoise and chicken feathers; right, Marshallese fan-likiep.

39. Kiki emon (sleep good) pillowcase made on Majuro—gift from Mrs. Joseph Goss.

40. Nien mani-child's or adult's purse.

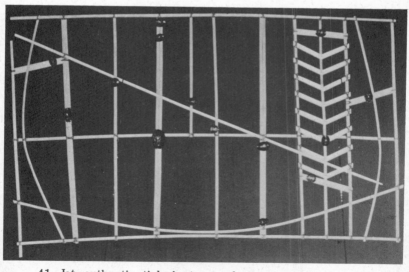

41. Jat—authentic stick chart; one of many types—Marshallese.

42. Marshallese outrigger canoe.

43. Black coral tree.

95

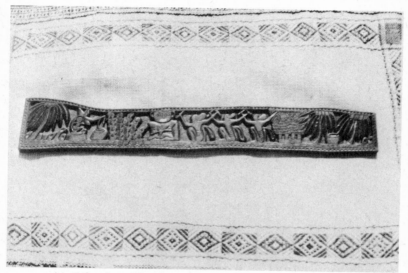

44. Tekeok and Imid—the woman who violated custom.

45. Magic breadfruit tree-carved in dort wood by O'Siik.

46. Storyboards from Palau.

47. Fish-shaped fish-bearing tree storyboard—Palau, Legend I.

97

48. Carved Dilukai woman with bowl—owned by Tony Mondello.

49. Man, eating beetlenut—Woman, with baby—Palau—lamps.

50. Story of Tabang, canoe in the Taro swamp.

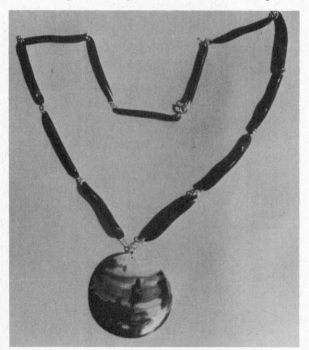

51. Black coral necklace—shell pendant— Palau—by Obak.

52. Man and woman headhunters—note comb in his hair.

53. Six-sided Dilukai abai.

54. Illengels—Medechihelau and Itungelbai—small vases owned by Carl and Thelma Blake.

55. Palauan money pot.

56. Tobi monkey men.

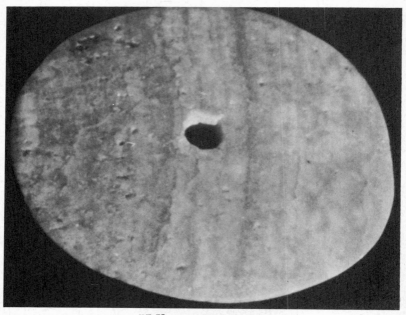

57. Yapese stone money.

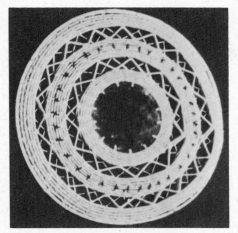

58. Fancy Truk coconut and tortoise basket.

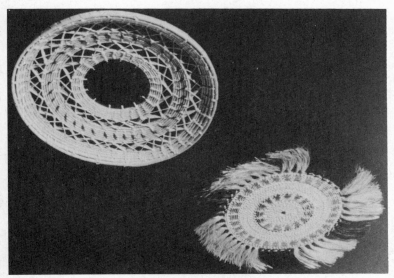

59. Trukese mats and baskets.

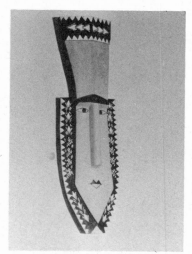

60. Mortlock devil mask.

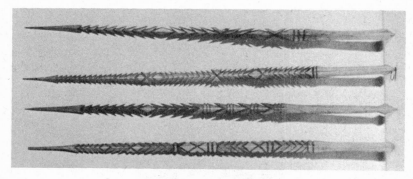

61. Trukese love sticks.

62. Letter opener—model gecko.

63. Kapingamarangi model canoe.

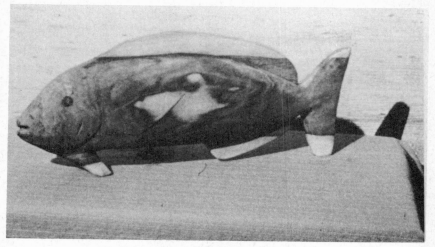

64. Model fish from Kapingamarangi village.

65. Coconut sakau jar.

66. Tortoise shell purse intertwined in pandanus and coconut fibers—made on Nukor, Caroline Islands.

67. Trochus hiloticus (tep shell).

68. Classic Kosrae fan.

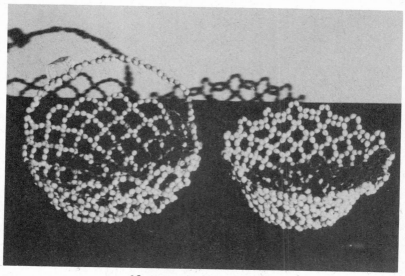

69. Saipan Job's tears baskets.

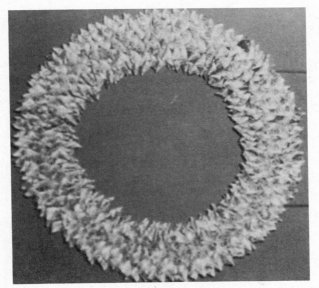

70. Tangen Tangen seed pod wreath—Saipan, Mariana Islands.

71. Tangen Tangen seed and pod necklace—and Kukui nut belt.

72. Saipanese seed saw.

73. Bo Jo Bo Doll from San Roque—Tana Rosa Guild—Saipan.

74. Photograph frame made of shells indigenous to Kwajalein Atoll—gift from Steve and Likijon Kelen.

Bibliography

Libokra—A reporter in Micronesia—E.J. Kahn, Jr.—Norton—1965-66.

Marshallese Stick Charts—Neal Hines and E.H. Bryan, Kwajalein Hourglass and Marshallese.

Legends of Storyboards—Palau Woodworker's Guild and Palau Storyteller.

Truk Love Stick Legend—Truk storytellers.

Ivory Nut—Tales of the South Pacific—James Michener and Ponape.

Bo Jo Bo Legend—Tana Rosa Guild—Saipan.

Island Statistics—High Commissioner's reports, Trust Territory Brochures, and Interior Department yearly reports.